Jeff Fountain

THE LITTLE TOWN

THAT BLESSED THE WORLD

YWAM Publishing

YWAM Publishing is the publishing ministry of Youth With A Mission. Youth With A Mission (YWAM) is an international missionary organization of Christians from many denominations dedicated to presenting Jesus Christ to this generation. To this end, YWAM has focused its efforts in three main areas: (1) training and equipping believers for their part in fulfilling the Great Commission (Matthew 28:19), (2) personal evangelism, and (3) mercy ministry (medical and relief work).

For a free catalog of books and materials, contact:

YWAM Publishing
PO Box 55787 Seattle, WA 98155
(425) 771-1153 or (800) 922-2143
www. ywampublishing.com

In Europe, contact:

bragghaus@yahoo .com
www. ywampublishing.eu
www. hfe.org

Copyright © 2007 by YWAM Publishing

Published by Youth With A Mission Publishing
PO Box 55787, Seattle, WA 98155

ISBN 13: 978-1-57658-453-8

Cover photography: Jennifer Bragg
Printing: WinterDruck Herrnhut
post@winterdruck.de
thomas.bragg@ winterdruck.de

Printed in Germany

•

This small book has been compiled
on the occasion of YWAM's *Festival of the Nations*,
coinciding with the 275th anniversary
of Modern Moravian Missions,
and to pay tribute to
the little town
that blessed the world.

•

CONTENTS

THE LITTLE TOWN
THAT
BLESSED THE WORLD

INTRODUCTION

FROM THE LOOKOUT TOWER OVERLOOKING THE CEMENTARY, visitors can survey the red-tiled roofs of the eighteenth-century German town of Herrnhut beyond the tree-tops.

Green and golden fields roll south toward pale blue mountains which border the Czech Republic. Look to the east and you will see a distant steam cloud billowing from a nuclear power station in Poland.

In the near distance, further to the left, rises the Berthelsdorf church steeple. Here, on one extraordinary August Wednesday morning in 1727, the Herrnhut community experienced a spiritual visitation. This little town, tucked away in the corner of Saxony and often unmarked on maps, has played a giant role in the unfolding story of the World Christian movement.

For Herrnhut was the vital link between the long tradition of the Ancient Moravian Church, or *Unitas Fratrum,*

7

and the Modern Moravian Church, reborn under the leadership of Count Nicolas Ludwig von Zinzendorf.

This booklet will take you in seven giant strides through church history from the first century to the twenty-first. We will follow a domino effect leading us from Jerusalem to Herrnhut, and then from Herrnhut to the ends of the earth.

We start with the *Apostle Paul,* who planted the first churches in Europe, including the fellowship in Thessalonica, Greece. From this Macedonian city, two brothers *Cyril and Methodius* later set out to take the gospel to the Slavs in Bohemia and Moravia, today's Czech Republic.

Centuries later *Jan Hus* agitated to bring reform and renewal to the church in Moravia, leading to the formation of a fully Protestant Church, the *Ancient Moravian Church.* This occurred fifty years before Luther's Reformation.

Jan Amos Comenius, one of the last bishops of this church, was forced into exile by religious wars and left writings about this ancient church, later to be discovered by *Count Ludwig von Zinzendorf.* These writings helped trigger the spiritual renewal of what came to be known as the *Modern Moravian Church.*

We will then read about *John Wesley's* life-changing encounter with Moravian missionaries and his visit to Herrnhut just prior to revival breaking out in England;

and how *William Carey* modeled his missionary community in Serampore, India, on Herrnhut.

Lastly we will pay tribute to how the community lifestyle of this little Saxon town has influenced the many missionary communities of the global movement founded by *Loren Cunningham,* YOUTH WITH A MISSION, the first mission to have been active in every country of the world.

This booklet has been published on the occasion of the *Festival of the Nations,* a gathering of YWAM staff from across Europe and around the world, held in Herrnhut and neighboring Ruppersdorf at Pentecost 2007.

This year also marks the 275th anniversary of when the first two Moravian missionaries, Leonard Dober and David Nitschmann, set out from this little town at three o'clock one August morning in 1732. Riding in Zinzendorf's carriage to Bautzen, they continued on foot to Copenhagen, and eventually by ship to the Caribbean island of Saint Thomas.

Tens of thousands around the world have since followed in their footsteps. Dober and Nitschmann themselves, were following in the footsteps of Paul the Missionary, which is where our story of this little Saxon town really begins...

Jeff Fountain
Pentecost 2007

PART I
• FROM JERUSALEM TO HERRNHUT •
• *33 AD* TO *1722* •

1. PAUL

FIRST MISSIONARY
TO EUROPE

· AD 10-65 ·

WHEN PAUL STEPPED ASHORE IN 'EUROPE' FOR THE FIRST TIME, AROUND THE YEAR AD50, HE HAD NO NOTION OF THE CONTINENT AS WE DO TODAY. THE CLASSICAL WORLD WAS SEEN AS A RING OF CIVILISATION BORDERING THE MEDITERRANEAN SEA. BEYOND THE ROMAN EMPIRE LAY THE WILD AND DANGEROUS REGIONS OF THE BARBARIANS.

Paul was a visionary. He had had several visions. One, on the Damascus Road, had totally transformed his life and personal future. Another, while traveling through what is today's western Turkey, had totally redirected his ministry. A 'European' had appeared one night in this vision and urged Paul to 'come across to Macedonia (northern Greece today) and help us'.

This second vision led directly to the planting of the first 'European' churches. He spent his first Sabbath on the continent with a handful of women on the riverbanks outside of Philippi. Yet even Paul the visionary probably had no inkling how the message he shared that day would eventually become the single greatest influence in shaping Europe's identity.

Innocent as this small band would have appeared to passersby, it quickly led to a public uproar. Paul, with Silas, delivered a slave-girl from a fortune-telling spirit. In turn, they were accused of disturbing the peace. Her owners brought charges, and the two men were flogged and imprisoned.

That night, God intervened yet again. As Paul and Silas were entertaining the other prisoners with their singing, there was a violent and convenient earthquake. Chains fell off. Doors swung open. And the greatest miracle of all: *the prisoners stayed put!* The hardened Roman jailer, realizing he was in the presence of holy men whom he had treated as common criminals, threw himself at their feet, asking, "What do I have to do to be saved?"

A pretty dramatic start to the church in Europe!

Similar divine interventions had occurred in Jerusalem less then two decades earlier, after the birth of the church at Pentecost. Angelic deliverances from prison on at least two occasions, speaking in tongues, flames nestling on the disciples' heads, bold proclamation by the previously timid Peter and others, instant healings of the lame, the sick and the blind, Ananias and Sapphira suddenly dropping dead, unity and community among the believers... and on the list goes!

The church was thus born in *suffering*, but also experienced *grace* and *glory*, as it would throughout the ages to come.

COOL RECEPTION

Paul's conversion, however, was one miracle the early Christians seemed reluctant to accept. That is understandable, for the young man known as Saul, a promising Pharisee student of Gamaliel, had watched in agreement as Stephen was dragged out of the city and stoned. "Saul entirely approved of the killing," Luke tells us in Acts 8:1, and adds two verses later that "Saul then worked for the total destruction of the Church."

It was Barnabas, 'son of encouragement', who had taken Saul the convert under his wing, when the rest of the Jerusalem leadership had doubted his sincerity. After his dramatic encounter with the Risen Jesus *en route* to Damascus, Saul had spent some three years as a desert recluse before making a two-week visit with Peter and James in Jerusalem (Galatians 1:17-18). After the rather cool reception there, Saul retreated back home to Tarsus ... to make tents!

Once again, it was Barnabas who came to Saul's rescue. He fetched him from Tarsus to help disciple young non-Jewish converts in Antioch. A cosmopolitan Jew, a Roman citizen schooled in Latin and Greek, Saul would understand the culture of these new *'Christ-ians'*, as they were being nick-named.

Who knows? Humanly speaking, had Barnabas not reached out to him, Saul may have spent the rest of his life in Tarsus tent-making. And the first missionary team of Barnabas and Saul would never have been sent off from Antioch to Cyprus. But Cyprus in fact was where Saul received new authority and a new name: we now read of *'Paul* and his companions' rather than 'Barnabas and Saul' (Acts 13:13).

RIOTS

Later unfortunately, Paul and Barnabas parted ways arguing over Barnabas' young nephew John Mark. The fact that the Gospel of Mark later came from this young man's pen suggests that Barnabas saw potential which Paul had missed.

So on Paul's second missionary journey, it was Silas who was his fellow prisoner in Philippi. Now, after their release, embarrassed officials begged them to leave town.

Their next stop was Thessalonica. Again their preaching led to riots, and a reputation of 'turning the whole world upside down'! Then, after three short weeks, Paul and Silas had to leave town, this time under the cover of darkness. Thessalonian Jews hounded them further on their travels, forcing them to keep moving on. Hardly ideal circumstances for church planting!

Further south in Corinth, Paul wrote his first epistle to the Thessalonians – the first written to any 'European' church. The second epistle he wrote a few months later to clarify some points from the first. The believers received Paul's instructions to *"be joyful always, pray continually, give thanks in all circumstances, and not to put out the Spirit's fire"* (I Thess. 5:16-19).

In this epistle Paul introduces themes of suffering, grace and glory, which he expands upon in later letters, e.g. to the Corinthians and to the Romans.

(See II Corinthians 4 and Romans 8).

The Thessalonian church, despite suffering and opposition, withstood the tests of time. Centuries later, it would produce two of the most influential missionaries Europe has ever known.

2. CYRIL &
METHODIUS

APOSTLES TO THE SLAVS
• CYRIL 827-868 • METHODIUS 825-885 •

WHEN THE REQUEST CAME FROM MORAVIA FOR MIS-SIONARIES, THE EMPEROR AND THE PATRIARCH KNEW IMMEDIATELY WHO TO SEND.

Prince Rastislav was asking them for teachers who could instruct his Moravian people about the gospel in their own language. The Moravians were a Slavic tribe who had migrated from the East and settled in and around today's Czech Republic.

Catholic missionaries already active in the prince's territory insisted that Moravians should use only Latin liturgy. But the prince disagreed. He wanted his people to understand their worship, so he had sent for help from the rulers in Constantinople.

After Paul had planted the first churches in what we now call Europe, the Christian message had spread quickly throughout the Roman Empire. It had circled the Mediterranean Sea and radiated out to pagan tribes – like the Slavs – settling into the European peninsular.

By the ninth century, Latin-speaking churches and communities were established in much of Western Europe. The bishop of Rome, the pope, was their spiritual leader. In the Greek-speaking east, Byzantium, the bishop of Constantinople was the spiritual leader. The three other patriarchs of the early church – in Jerusalem, Antioch and Alexandria – were now all living under Muslim rule.

East and West had begun to drift apart. Tensions over doctrine and leadership were mounting and in the year 1054 would erupt into the Great Schism – a split that would scar Europe's spiritual, social and political history for another thousand years.

BROTHERS

In response to the prince's request then, Emperor Michael III and Patriarch Photius agreed to send two experienced priests with exceptional language and diplomatic skills. Methodius (825-885) and his younger brother, Constantine (827-868) – later renamed Cyril – had grown up in Thessalonica, where the first European church had been planted by Paul nearly 800 years before.

Both already had careers behind them as priests and monks. They had also been missionaries among the Khazars in the Dnieper-Volga region. Constantine had been a professor of philosophy and had also served as a librarian in Constantinople's famous Santa Sophia cathedral. Methodius had governed a district settled by Slavs and had already learned to speak their unwritten language.

So when they set off for Moravia in 863, they brought the skills needed for a task complicated by the growing East-West tensions around language and authority. For on Christmas Day in the year 800, the pope in Rome had unexpectedly crowned the Frankish ruler Charlemagne as emperor. This had been a shrewd action – it implied the emperor owed his title to the Church and so ensured the empire's loyalty to the Church. Empire and Church thus worked together to expand the eastern border of Charlemagne's rule among the Slavs in Moravia.

The first task the brothers set for themselves was to create a Slavic alphabet in order to give the Moravians the Bible in their own language. While Rome imposed Latin conformity of language and culture, the eastern churches used the local languages. Barnabas and Paul, it was argued, had not required the first Greek Christians in Antioch to worship and read in Hebrew. They had affirmed the need for believers to pray and worship in their own language. Another predecessor to Methodius and Constantine, Ulfilas (c.310-388), had also created a Gothic alphabet for the Goths. Even earlier (301), the Armenians in the Caucasus region had had the Scriptures and the liturgy in their native language.

Methodius and Constantine reasoned: *"If God sends sunlight, air and rain to all the peoples, this is to testify that God loves all people in the same way. Why do you think then that God wants to be praised only in the languages of three peoples?" (Hebrew, Greek and Latin).*

Using Greek and Hebrew letters, the brothers thus developed a 43 letter 'Slavonic' alphabet to produce the first Slavic Bible and liturgy.

Friction with Roman missionaries was inevitable. When it came, they decided to travel to Rome in 868 to see the pope. Adrian II received them warmly. Constantine entered a monastery during their stay in the city, taking on the name of Cyril – by which he is remembered today.

But Cyril's stay in the monastery was literally short-lived. For, just weeks after arriving in Rome, he suddenly died. Methodius had to return to Moravia alone to carry on the work. Thankfully, Adrian II had appointed him as archbishop and authorized him to use the Slavonic liturgy.

After his return however, circumstances went from bad to worse. Prince Rastislav who had originally invited the brothers also died. His successor did not share Rastivlav's opinion to worship in the local language, and threw Methodius into prison. After two long years, he was released by a new pope, but forbidden to use the Slavonic liturgy. In 878 he was then summoned to Rome on charges of heresy. However, he managed to convince the pope he was not a heretic and was allowed to return to Moravia, freely using the Slavonic liturgy until his death in 885.

A new bishop was appointed to replace Methodius, but one of his first acts outlawed the Slavonic liturgy and Bible once more.

Persecution forced Methodius' followers into exile. Many moved south to Bulgaria and reorganized a Slavic-speaking church. A school was established on the shores of Lake Ochrid. Clement, one of the brothers' disciples, further refined the Slavonic alphabet into what is known as the Cyrillic Alphabet, named in honor of Cyril. Today it is still used throughout the Slavic world.

From there the Cyrillic liturgy and scriptures spread to Romania, Serbia, Croatia, Moldova, the Ukraine, Lithuania and Russia.

But for the Moravians, the longing to worship in their own language never died...

3. JAN HUS

REFORMER & MARTYR

• 1369-1415 •

THE CROWD PACKED INTO THE BETHLEHEM CHAPEL LIS-TENED IN RAPT SILENCE TO THE CLEAR, BOLD VOICE OF JAN HUS. HE WAS PREACHING AND READING THE BIBLE IN THEIR OWN MOTHER TONGUE.

The Church of Rome strongly disapproved of any departure from Latin liturgy. But Hus, Rector of the University of Prague, had emerged as a popular champion for Church reform and Biblical authority. The cavernous 'chapel' in the town center, able to seat 3000 people, had been built by Jan of Milheim to be used for worship on one condition: that services be held in the Moravian language.

Young Bohemians studying at Oxford in England had brought back to Prague John Wycliffe's teachings, that the Bible had authority over church tradition. This early English reformer (d.1384) had bravely overcome much opposition to give the English people the Bible in their own language.

Wycliffe's teachings resonated with Hus who knew well the long spiritual history of his own people reaching back to the pioneering efforts of Cyril and Methodius. Since the ninth century, however, Rome's policy had been to impose the Latin liturgy and to forbid worship in the local languages. Religion for ordinary people had remained mystical and unintelligible. (Hence the phrase 'hocus pocus', corrupted from: 'hoc est corpus meum' – 'this is my body'.)

Hus believed much more needed reforming in the church of the day. In 1411 the new Pope John XXIII had introduced the selling of indulgences, for the forgiveness of sins, in order to finance his wars. Almost every church in Prague had large chests to collect indulgence monies. But not the Bethlehem Chapel. Instead, quoting Scripture and foreshadowing Luther, Hus expounded: "A man can receive the pardon of his sins only through the power of God and by the merits of Christ."

'INVITATION'

Hus saw the church as corrupted by wealth and power. Three rivals claimed to be pope. One was later suspected of having another murdered! A general council was called for in the free city of Constance, today on the border of Switzerland and Germany, to address such concerns. Hus was soon to receive an 'invitation' to attend this council.

Born into a peasant family from Bohemia – the southern part of today's Czech Republic – Hus had studied for the priesthood and was first chosen to become a professor and then the faculty dean. At the age of thirty-three, he became rector of the University of Prague! That same year he was chosen to be the preacher in the Bethlehem Chapel.

Queen Sophia often worshipped at the chapel and King Wenzel ordered papal agents to let him preach in peace. But that didn't prevent Hus from being placed under 'the ban' and soon thereafter being excommunicated by the pope. Church officials publicly burned two hundred volumes of Wycliffe's books. Protesters were beheaded in the street. Hus had to leave the city and began preaching throughout the countryside to large crowds for a year and a half.

When news of the council in Constance reached Prague, the king's son, Sigismund, suggested Hus should present his case for reform there. Many warned him not to go, but the prince guaranteed his safety. In November 1414 Hus arrived at the 'Holy Synod of Constance', a colorful and festive event with cardinals, patriarchs, archbishops, bishops, electors, princes, dukes, counts, barons, musicians and entertainers – and the pope of course – all witnessed by a crowd of 50,000.

Summoned to meet with some cardinals, Hus was promptly thrown into a dungeon, despite all guarantees to the contrary. Appeals from nobility back in Bohemia fell on deaf ears. The cardinals replied that promises to heretics did not need to be honored.

After a month of trials, Hus was found guilty on thirty counts of heresy. A thousand soldiers guarded the great procession as Hus was taken outside the city, and burned at the stake on July 6, 1415.

A week before his death, Hus wrote from jail to the masters, bachelors and students of Prague University: "Stand on the recognized truth which prevails over all and retains its power until the end of time."

In 1999, on the eve of the new millennium, a symposium was held in the Vatican on 'Master Jan Hus', which led to his reinstatement and an official Catholic apology for his execution. Vaclav Havel, then president of the Czech Republic, said: "for hundreds of years, the name of master Jan Hus has been inscribed in the mind of the nation, especially for his deep love of truth." Hus' motto, *Veritas omnia vincit* (Truth prevails), had become the national Czech motto, *Pravda vitez*. That motto, continued Havel, became the cry of the Velvet Revolution, which brought down the communist regime.

Today in the Old Town Square of Prague, the bronze figure of Jan Hus stands tall as a hero of the Czech nation. But the story does not end here. Fifty years before Luther's Reformation, Hus' followers organized themselves into the first truly Protestant church, the *Unitas Fratrum*.

And when the Reformation did break out across Europe, both Luther and Calvin recognized the trailblazing work of Jan Hus.

"If only we had listened to the Bohemian doctor!" lamented Calvin.

4. Jan Amos Comenius

Father of

Modern Education

JAN
AMOS
KOMENSKY

1592 - 1670

IN THE BACK STREETS OF THE SMALL DUTCH TOWN OF NAARDEN, JUST OUTSIDE OF AMSTERDAM, IS THE MODEST MAUSOLEUM OF A MAN KNOWN GLOBALLY AS THE 'FATHER OF MODERN EDUCATION'. FEW EUROPEANS RECOGNISE HIS NAME BUT ANY CZECH WOULD PROUDLY TESTIFY THAT JAN AMOS COMENIUS IS THEIR GREATEST NATIONAL HERO, NEXT TO JAN HUS.

Although born in Moravia, the tumultuous times in which he lived steered him from country to country and finally to Amsterdam in Holland, where he spent the last decade of his life.

Comenius' parents had died when he was still young. As members of the Brethren, they traced their roots back to the Hussites, followers of Jan Hus. Decades after his martyrdom in 1415, the Hussites had formed their own church, the *Unitas Fratrum,* or Unity of the Brethren. They took this step only after sending out emissaries in a vain attempt to find existing churches to which they could join themselves. Also called the Ancient Moravian Church, it was in fact a Protestant Church, half a century before Luther!

When the Reformation broke out, led by Luther, Zwingli and Calvin, creating a huge upheaval in the spiritual landscape of German- and French-speaking Europe, the Brethren rose up on the side of the Reformers.

Comenius (or *Komensky* in Slavic) was a young teacher of 26 years in 1618 when his country became embroiled in the Thirty Years War. This war was part of the drawn-out struggle between the forces of the Reformation and the Counter-Reformation. Protestant nobles revolted, but at the Battle of White Mountain in 1620, the Catholic House of Hapsburg was victorious. Bohemia and Moravia were now firmly under Catholic control.

OPTIONS

The Brethren found themselves on the losing side. They had few options: recant, be killed, go underground, or leave the country.

Already on several occasions, Comenius had had to flee from hostile soldiers. In one such flight his wife and a child had died. All his written manuscripts hidden under the floorboards of his house had gone up in flames.

With the Brethren now scattered by persecution, Comenius found himself in 1628 shepherding a small straggling band of refugees across the mountainous border to safety in Poland. As they stopped to take one last look back at their homeland, Comenius prayed for God to preserve a 'hidden seed' in that land that would one day glorify God's name.

The refugees were welcomed in Lissa (now Lezno in Poland), which became a 'center in exile' for the *Unitas Fratrum*. Comenius was consecrated as bishop and appointed head of the college the Brethren established there. He remarried, with the daughter of another bishop, and enjoyed two peaceful decades writing and developing further his educational ideas.

And very progressive they were. Education should be made available for all, rich and poor, girls and boys, he insisted. *"The teacher must be kind and fatherly, must give both praise and reward, and must always, where possible, give the children something to look at,"* he wrote.

All knowledge, he believed, was integrated in God's Truth. Since everything would be reconciled together in Christ, he taught, there was a comprehensive cohesion to all wisdom. All truth was God's truth. Comenius developed this idea into what he called *Pansophy* (all wisdom), based on Colossians 1:28 - *'we proclaim Him, admonishing and teaching everyone with all wisdom.'*

In a truly radical innovation, Comenius developed the world's first picture book for children, a concept taken for granted today. Learning should happen through all the senses, he believed, not just rote learning. It should be experiential as well as cognitive. He took children on 'field-trips' to the local blacksmith to let them hold the hammer and smite the molten metal themselves.

INVITATIONS

From Poland, Comenius' reputation as an educator began to attract invitations. Oliver Cromwell asked him to come to England to reorganize education, and Parliament considered founding a college for him there before civil war interrupted such plans. Governor Winthrop of Massachusetts invited him to become the first president of Harvard College but he preferred to stay closer to his flock in

Poland. With Queen Christina's help, he engaged in school reforms throughout Sweden, hoping in vain to gain support for the Brethren in Bohemia. He visited other scattered Brethren in Hungary and Transylvania (modern Romania).

When Protestant Sweden invaded Poland in 1655 and suffered defeat, Catholic fury was pent on the Protestant community in Lissa. Once again Comenius lost his library and manuscripts and he was forced to flee. He was offered refuge in Amsterdam. There he continued to help his scattered flock, printing new Bohemian Bibles, and adding to the over 150 titles in his name. One of his last projects was to update his history of the Brethren, called *The Order of Discipline.* This book, we shall see, would be a key link in the rebirth of the Ancient Moravian Church.

A statue outside the old walls of Naarden symbolizes the honor, in which Comenius has continued to be held by believer and non-believer alike. Given by the then communist government of Czechoslovakia, it recognizes the nation's famous son as 'a world reformer in education, literature and philosophy'.

His noble image is also etched on Czech currency – both the old twenty koruna communist variety and the new two hundred koruna post-Communist issue – embossed, in fine print, with the words:

> *Jan Amos Komensky 1592-1670.*

PART II
• **FROM HERRNHUT TO THE ENDS OF THE EARTH** •
•*1722 TO 2007* •

5. Count von Zinzendorf

Humble Nobleman

• 1700-1760 •

AS THE YEAR 1727 OPENED, THE LITTLE TOWN OF
HERRNHUT WAS A NEST OF QUARRELLING AND BICKER-
ING DISSIDENTS. THE ORIGINAL RAG-TAG BUNCH OF
REFUGEES HAD BEEN ALLOWED TO SETTLE ON A ROLLING
HILLSIDE, CLOSE TO WHERE GERMANY, POLAND AND
TODAY'S CZECH REPUBLIC MEET. OVER FIVE YEARS IT
HAD GROWN INTO A RELIGIOUS HAVEN FOR SEPARATISTS
AND EXILES FROM MANY BACKGROUNDS: CATHOLIC, RE-
FORMED, ANABAPTIST AND LUTHERAN, AS WELL AS
MORAVIAN.

Dissidents by nature are strong-willed and discord was
to be expected. The initial settlers were descendants of
Hussites, followers of Jan Hus. Their roots were in the
Unitas Fratrum, the Ancient Moravian Church, dating
back to 1457. Catholic domination of Bohemia and
Moravia forced the Brethren underground, or, as with
Comenius, over the border to Poland.

Those who stayed behind continued to worship in secret.
They never stopped praying for the revival of their
church and the restoration of free worship.

Christian David, a young Moravian Catholic, came to
personal faith in Jesus while working in Görlitz, Silesia
(on today's German-Polish border). At great personal
risk, David returned home to tell others about Jesus and
to help the Brethren find refuge.

One day, back in Silesia, he met a young Saxon nobleman
named Count Nicolas Ludwig von Zinzendorf. After
hearing David's story and of the plight of the Moravian
Brethren, the Count offered for them to settle temporarily
on his own estate near Berthelsdorf. David wasted no

time immediately rushing to his friends and bringing them back under the cover of darkness across the border into Saxony.

HAVEN

There they began to chop down trees to build houses. Zinzendorf's steward updated the absent Count about the new construction on the slopes of the Hutberg (Watch Hill), and wished for the town to 'abide under the Lord's Watch' (*Herrnhut*).

Soon refugees from other backgrounds heard of the 'safe haven' and joined the original Moravians. Arguments about communion, liturgy, pastoral oversight and relationship to the local Lutheran church began to sow dissension. One newcomer named Krüger even called the Count 'The Beast', and Pastor Rothe, from the Lutheran Church in nearby Berthelsdorf, the 'False Prophet'.

The fledgling community threatened to fall apart. But early in the new year of 1727, Krüger suffered a breakdown and left. At this point, the 26-year-old Count stepped in to restore harmony and give leadership to Herrnhut.

Zinzendorf himself was Lutheran and had studied at the Pietistic school in Halle. As a 15-year-old, he and some friends had formed *'The Order of the Mustard Seed'*, a sort of spiritual knighthood pledged to love the whole human family. Among those who later joined this order were Archbishop Potter of Canterbury, Cardinal de Noailles of Paris, Governor Oglethorpe of Georgia and King Christian VI of Denmark.

While on his Grand Tour of European cities as part of his aristocratic grooming, young Zinzendorf had been greatly moved by a painting of the crucifixion in a gallery in Düsseldorf, Germany. Under the title *Ecco Homo,* he read the words: *All this I did for you; what will you do for me?*

A decade later, Zinzendorf now realized what his Savior wanted him to do. Taking furlough from state duties, he began visiting each family in the Herrnhut community, just across the fields from his own homestead. As winter gave way to spring, the Count won their trust and rekindled a spirit of unity. Eventually all the people signed a Brotherly Agreement, stating that:

Herrnhut shall stand in unceasing love with all children of God in all Churches, criticize none, take part in no quarrel against those differing in opinion, except to preserve for itself the evangelical purity, simplicity and grace.

By the summer, a new spirit of prayer had developed in the community. Meanwhile Zinzendorf chanced across a book in the library of Zittau by a man whose name his settlers had often mentioned: *Comenius.* As he scanned the pages of *The Order of Discipline*, he began to realize he was reading the story of the very people now living on *his* estate! *Now* he could understand why they were longing for the restoration of their church – and what his own role should be in that renewal. With great anticipation, he returned to Herrnhut to share his discovery.

FELLOWSHIP

By now everyone was sensing God was doing something new. Pastor Rothe invited the whole community to the

Lord's Table on Wednesday, August 13. Zinzendorf visited each member of the community to prepare their hearts for the first time of communion since the months of discord.

Even as Pastor Rothe began the service, some started praising and weeping. God the Holy Spirit was clearly present in a deep and special way. Confession and forgiveness flowed. And when the service officially ended, clusters of communicants continued to fellowship together, savoring God's presence. *'From this day on'*, wrote one historian, *'Herrnhut became a living congregation of Jesus Christ.'*

The new unity was expressed in a community lifestyle of worship, servanthood, love feasts, foot-washing ceremonies, and a 24-hour prayer chain began and was unbroken for over one hundred years! The Herrnhut residents began to receive in prayer a big vision of God's heart for the unreached peoples of the world.

Five years later, this small community of refugees began to send out missionaries to the Caribbean and Surinam, to Lapland and Greenland, to Morocco and South Africa, to Russia and Turkey, to Georgia and to Pennsylvania. By the time Zinzendorf died in 1760, it is said that this revived Moravian Church had done more for world missions than all the other protestant churches combined.

As they began spreading out across the world, they greatly influenced and inspired others. One was a young English clergyman sailing to America, whose encounter with Moravian missionaries on board the ship was to have global consequences....

6. JOHN WESLEY

APOSTLE TO ENGLAND
• 1703-1791 •

'THE WINDS ROARED ROUND ABOUT US, AND WHISTLED AS DISTINCTLY AS IF IT HAD BEEN A HUMAN VOICE. THE SHIP NOT ONLY ROCKED TO AND FRO WITH THE UTMOST VIOLENCE, BUT SHOOK AND JARRED WITH SO UNEQUAL GRATING, A MOTION THAT ONE COULD NOT BUT WITH GREAT DIFFICULTY KEEP ONE'S HOLD OF ANYTHING, NOR STAND A MOMENT WITHOUT IT. EVERY TEN MINUTES CAME A SHOCK AGAINST THE STERN OR SIDE OF THE SHIP, WHICH ONE WOULD THINK SHOULD DASH THE PLANKS TO PIECES.'

So wrote John Wesley in his journal January 25, 1736. He was describing the violent, mid-Atlantic storm, which almost sank the ship carrying him and his brother Charles to the new colony of Georgia in America.

Neither John nor Charles lacked religious zeal. At Oxford University, studying for the Anglican priesthood, they had started a Bible club with fellow student George Whitefield. Others disparagingly called them the *'Holy Club'*, *'Bible moths'*, *'Enthusiasts'*, and other derogatory names. The name that stuck was *'Methodists'*, which mocked their disciplined, liturgical and methodical lifestyle of doing good works.

Yet on this voyage John saw what he did lack.

Among the 150 passengers caught in that storm on board the *Simmonds,* were twenty-four Moravian missionaries. Four years after the first missionaries had set out from Herrnhut, they too were being sent out to reinforce a new Moravian settlement in Georgia. On the ship, the missionaries had greatly impressed Wesley by their humility, servanthood and readiness to do tasks refused by the English passengers.

VAIN WORDS

Seeking comfort in the wild of the storm, Wesley had joined the Moravians for prayers. *'In the midst of the psalm wherewith their service began,'* so his journal reads, *'the sea broke over, split the mainsail in pieces, covered the ship, and poured in between the decks, as if the great deep had already swallowed us up. A terrible screaming began among the English. The Germans calmly sung on. I asked one of them afterward, "Were you not afraid?" He answered, "I thank God, no." I asked, "But were not your women and children afraid?" He replied mildly, "No; our women and children are not afraid to die."'*

Later Wesley wrote: *'I went to America to convert the Indians, but oh, who shall convert me? I have a fair summer religion. I can talk well ... when no danger is near. But let death look me in the face, and my spirit is troubled. Nor can I say, "to die is gain."'*

This was the first of a series of encounters with Moravians, which would lead to perhaps one of the most significant conversions in history.

On landing, Wesley met the leader of the Moravian settlement in Georgia, Augustus Spangenberg. "My brother," said Spangenberg, "I must first ask you one or two questions. Have you the witness within yourself? Does the Spirit of God bear witness with you that you are a child of God?" Wesley evaded the question. "Do you know Jesus Christ?" pressed Spangenberg. "I know," replied Wesley, "that He is the Savior of the world." "Do you know that He has saved you?" persisted Spangenberg further. "I hope He has died to save me," Wesley fended. "Do you know yourself?" "I do," replied Wesley. But he confessed in his journal: "I fear they were vain words."

Later in 1738, back in London, Wesley met yet another Moravian traveling to Georgia, Peter Boehler. Unimpressed by Wesley's religiosity, the 26-year-old Boehler said: "My brother, my brother, that philosophy of yours must be purged away." When John Wesley complained, "how can I preach a 'faith', which I have not got?" Boehler answered: "Preach 'faith' till you have it, and then, because you have it, you will preach it."

Just a few weeks later, an unwilling Wesley made his way to Aldersgate Street to attend a Moravian Bible study. As Luther's preface to Romans was being read aloud, Wesley experienced his 'heart being strangely warmed'. This was the moment; he later recorded, when he received saving faith. Now he knew that Christ had indeed died for his sins, he wrote in his journal, that Jesus was indeed his personal savior.

Anxious to learn more about Moravian spirituality, he set out with companions to visit Herrnhut. He was not disappointed. *'The spirit of the brethren is above our highest expectation,'* he wrote back to Charles. *'Young and old, they breathe nothing but faith and love at all times and in all places.'* After leaving what he called 'this happy place', he wrote: *'I would gladly have spent my life here... O, when shall this Christianity cover the earth, as the waters cover the sea?'*

New Years Eve saw the Wesley's, Whitefield and several old Oxford Methodist friends joining sixty Moravians at the Fetter Lane Society, to pray in the new year of 1739. *'About three in the morning,'* wrote Wesley, *'the power of God came mightily upon us, insomuch that many cried for exceeding joy, and many fell to the ground.'*

This prayer meeting signaled the start of the Evangelical Revival. Under the leadership of John, Charles and George, was to take the message of salvation by faith to the working classes of Britain.

Following the Moravian model, Wesley and Whitefield set up bands and societies to disciple their converts. Wesley became a familiar figure on horseback riding the equivalent of ten times around the world!

Wesley's passion to see the lordship of Christ applied to every nook and cranny of society resulted in reforms and institutions taken for granted today: including the abolition of slavery, workers rights, trade unions, women's emancipation, education for all, the reform of prisons, hospitals and the nursing profession. Not without just cause has Wesley been called the Apostle of England.

In time, this renewal was to have global consequences. It birthed the Evangelical movement, and later led to the Salvation Army, the holiness, Pentecostal and charismatic movements – and, as we will see in the next chapter, the *modern missionary movement*.

7. WILLIAM CAREY

FATHER OF MODERN MISSIONS

• 1761–1834 •

"SEE WHAT THE MORAVIANS HAVE DONE! CAN WE NOT FOLLOW THEIR EXAMPLE, AND IN OBEDIENCE TO OUR HEAVENLY MASTER GO OUT INTO THE WORLD AND PREACH THE GOSPEL TO THE HEATHEN?"

With these words, thirty-year-old William Carey threw down copies of a magazine onto the table in front of his fellow Baptist ministers. It was England's first missionary magazine, reporting on Moravian missions around the world: *Periodical Accounts Relating to the Missions of the Church of the United Brethren.*

Baptists however looked on such efforts as human attempts to interfere with God's sovereignty, a 'profane outstretching of the hand to help the ark of God'. Objections were many. The time was not ripe. The means were not available. Distances were too far. The dangers were too great. The Great Commission was only for the first apostles. Missions should start at home.

So when Carey proposed that at a future meeting of Baptist pastors they should consider taking concrete steps to reach out to the worlds unreached, a senior pastor curtly told him: "Sit down, young man!" And added: "If God wants to save the heathen, he will do it without your help or mine!"

Carey did sit down – and started to write. What he penned became a sort of 'Magna Carta of Modern Missions', called *An Enquiry into the Obligation of Christians to use Means for the Conversion of the Heathen.* In its five sections, Carey countered all the usual arguments against missions, showing that the Great Commission was not only for the original disciples, but for every generation.

To those who argued that 'we ought not to force our way, but to wait for the openings and leadings of Providence' or, that too many natural obstacles blocked the way, he wrote: *'Have not the missionaries of the Unitas Fratrum, or Moravian Brethren, encountered the scorching heat of Abyssinia, and the frozen climes of Greenland, and Labrador, their difficult languages, and savage manners?'*

To others who stressed the dangers to life and limb from any contact with savages, Carey suggested that most reported barbarities had been provoked by offensive behavior. He noted that *'the Moravian missionaries have been very seldom molested. Nay, in general the heathen have chewed a willingness to hear the word; and have principally expressed their hatred of Christianity on account of the vices of nominal Christians.'*

SHOEMAKER

William Carey was born in 1761, nearly three decades after the first missionaries had set out from Herrnhut, and seven years before Captain Cook sailed off on his first voyage to the Pacific.

Despite his humble beginnings in the village of Hackleton near Northampton as an apprentice shoemaker, Carey set out to educate himself while working on his customers shoes. When about eighteen, he became a keen believer, leaving his nominal participation in the Anglican Church to become a Baptist. He taught himself Latin, Greek and Hebrew, as well as several modern languages.

Maps fascinated young Carey. He made himself a leather globe which he later used when teaching geography in Moulton on Northampton's outskirts, where he also pastored a small Baptist fellowship. As he traced Cook's voyages on this globe, his awareness of the world outside the knowledge of the gospel grew into a compelling obsession.

On the wall of his workshop he created a huge world map, pasting sheets of paper together to represent every country of the known world. Handwritten notes on the map recorded the populations of the various continents. Of the 730 million inhabitants of the world, Carey noted, more than 400 million were pagans, and 130 million were *Mohammedans* (Muslims).

However, every effort to convince his peers of the church's duty to attempt the spread of the Gospel among heathen nations was met with skepticism or outright opposition. In 1789, he moved 30 miles northwards to pastor in Leicester. That same year, the first edition of *Periodical Accounts* of Moravian missionaries appeared, greatly encouraging Carey in his obsession.

But three more years would pass before Carey had opportunity to address the whole Baptist Association, meeting in Nottingham. His sermon, based on Isaiah 54:2-3, argued that God's sovereignty did not negate man's responsibility. *'Expect great things from God!'* he preached, adding, *'Attempt great things for God.'*

Five months later, in October 1792, Carey and some of his friends set up the Baptist Missionary Society. Eager to practice what he preached, Carey volunteered to be the first missionary. The following year, he embarked with his family on the arduous five-month voyage to India, never to return to England.

Others came to join him: John Fountain[1] in 1796, William Ward and Joshua Marshman in 1799. Once more Carey looked to the Moravians for inspiration. He planned to set up a settlement in the Danish colony of Serampore, near Calcutta. Thirty years earlier, a Moravian community had been attempted there at the request of the Danish authorities, but without success. This did not discourage Carey, however, from modeling his own mission community directly on Herrnhut's principles: common possessions, shared purse, equality of station for missionary and convert alike, bound by a brotherly agreement. Following the Moravian pattern, Serampore would be a community of Christians living by their own industry, demonstrating the love of Christ to the pagan neighbors.

So began one of the most remarkable mission careers in history, inspiring the start of many new mission societies, and thousands from Europe and America would follow his example over the next decades.

Carey, the father of modern missions, had a vision that extended far beyond evangelism and church planting. It embraced the transformation of a whole nation. Not only would Carey become the founder of the Indian protestant church. Some say he became the central character in the story of the modernization of India – a story rooted in a little town in Saxony.

---

[1] the author's great-great-great-grandfather

8. LOREN CUNNINGHAM

PIONEER OF YOUTH MISSIONS

• 1935- •

'THERE ARE SO MANY OTHERS, IN OTHER CHURCHES AND GROUPS, WHO ARE ON THIS GREAT PILGRIMAGE OF WITNESS TO JESUS CHRIST, WHEREVER THEY MAY BE. THERE IS A FINE YOUTH ORGANIZATION CALLED YOUTH WITH A MISSION, CARRYING ON SUCH A WITNESS IN MISSION ONE WOULD THINK ONE WAS BACK IN THE OLD DAYS OF THE MORAVIAN CHURCH. IN FACT, THEY ACKNOWLEDGE OUR HISTORY IN MISSIONS AS PART OF THEIR INSPIRATION.'

–You Are My Witnesses, by Bishop James Weingarth, published to mark the 250th anniversary of Moravian missions in 1982, p.115.

Loren Cunningham knew little about the Herrnhut story in 1960 when he started YOUTH WITH A MISSION. Unlike William Carey who was directly inspired by the Moravian example, Loren only later learned about the many affinities between the Moravians and the youth missions movement he founded.

In 1956, as a twenty-year-old, Loren saw a literal vision of young people going out into the world like waves covering all the continents, showing the love of Jesus in word and deed. He understood that God was calling him to train and send young people as missionaries to all the nations.

God had always used young people throughout both the Bible and history, argued Loren. Joseph, Samuel, David, Esther and Daniel were all children or teenagers as they developed their relationship with God and were used to disciple nations. Most of the disciples were in their teens or twenties when Jesus called them to follow him. Timothy, Mark and others were engaged in missions with Paul as teenagers or young people.

But many said it couldn't and shouldn't be done; it was irresponsible to send out inexperienced, untrained youth into strange cultures and remote places.

How encouraging it was, therefore, when Loren and other YWAMers later began to discover how the Herrnhut community had championed the cause of young people! The Moravians believed children could hear God's voice, be called for missions, and engage in evangelism and intercession.

Zinzendorf himself was only fifteen years old when he and his friends established the *Order of the Mustard Seed*. He was twenty-two when Herrnhut was established, twenty-seven in the year of the renewal, and thirty-two when they sent out the first missionaries. Anna Nitschmann was also fifteen when she was elected an elder of the Herrnhut community, and eighteen when she was temporary leader of the whole community!

The spiritual outpouring of the summer of 1727 included the 'children's revival', when the earnest prayer-life of eleven-year-old Susanna Kuehnel prompted other children to go out into the fields to pray.

LOVE FEASTS

Loren had first heard snippets of the Moravian story when visiting St Thomas Island in the Caribbean in 1965, the very first Moravian mission field. He was greatly impressed by reports that early Moravian missionaries were prepared to sell themselves into bonded labor in order to work and witness among the slaves.

Six years later, a small YWAM team traveling in northern Czechoslovakia met some Czech Brethren who introduced them to an old Moravian tradition of the Love Feast. Returning to the Lausanne training center to share with Loren and others about this tradition, the team members still knew nothing about Herrnhut where this tradition began, just across the Czech-German border.

They were yet to discover the story of the spiritual outpouring in the Berthelsdorf church, when Zinzendorf had sent a message back to the kitchen in Herrnhut to prepare food baskets. The Count had wanted to encourage those still praying with one another to continue fellowshipping over a meal. This impromptu meal had become a weekly Love Feast, a central event in Herrnhut community life. Children's Love Feasts were also held regularly.

So too, the concept of a creative candle-light Love Feast, leading into prayer and worship to prepare for the Sabbath, spread from Lausanne to other YWAM centers.

HEROES

The main impact of the Moravian story on YWAM, however, came still later in 1975. Dr Charles Ringma, the speaker at a staff conference at the Heidebeek community in Holland, held his audience in rapt attention as he unfolded the Moravian story from Cyril and Methodius through Hus and Comenius to Zinzendorf and Wesley.

His listeners recognized how so many elements of the story resonated with the emerging YWAM community lifestyle: *small groups, accountability, 'body-life', worship, love feasts, foot-washing ceremonies, the championing of children, youth and women, seeking God for specific guidance, servanthood leadership, hospitality, intercession and a passion for missions...*

Dr Ringma's talk circulated on tape and as a magazine article among the growing number of YWAM centers, stirring much excitement. Here was a model from history of the kind of movement YWAM aspired to be – an example to follow, heroes to emulate!

Zinzendorf's commitment to an ecumenism of the heart, and to unity with diversity, became a guide for relationships within YWAM and with various church traditions. One Moravian slogan in particular entered YWAM phraseology: *In essentials, unity;*
in non-essentials, diversity;
in all things, charity.

Over the years the Moravian story has been a continuing source of inspiration to staff and students around the world. To tap into this rich heritage, Jan and Ute Schlegel of YWAM Germany, sensed a call to establish a new center in Herrnhut. In July 2004, the Schlegel's and their small team persevered in faith to purchase for YWAM the *Wasserschloss*, a small castle just outside of town, **debt-free**. Today, this former Red-Cross children's home, prepares young international students to go to the unreached peoples of the world, literally in the footsteps of the early Moravian missionaries.

As Zinzendorf led out in personal example by going to the nations himself, so too, did Loren recently fulfill his personal goal to visit and pray in every nation. Through his leadership example, and in no small measure inspired by the Moravians, YWAM has become the first mission to be active in every nation of the world.

EPILOGUE

Today we stand on the shoulders of many faithful men and women such as those we have read about in this book. Like the heroes of the faith recorded in Hebrews chapter 11, they too were persecuted, rejected, beaten, imprisoned, burnt at the stake, hunted, derided, misunderstood... and yet remained true to God's mission for their lives and for His world.

Because of their obedience, we have received a rich inheritance. Yet our 'prodigal generation' is squandering this inheritance rapidly, with little awareness of how and at what cost we have received the freedoms and values we enjoy today.

This book is a challenge to us not to forget, and a reminder of how God wants to use each of us, however humble our circumstances, to bless the world around us.

SOURCES AND RECOMMENDED FURTHER READING:

- *CAREY, CHRIST AND CULTURAL TRANSFORMATION*
  Vishal and Ruth Mangalwadi
  OM Publishing, 1997

- *COUNT ZINZENDORF*
  Janet & Geoff Benge
  YWAM Publishing, 2006

- *COUNT ZINZENDORF*
  John Weinlick
  Abingdon, 1956

- *SHAPERS OF OUR MODERN TIMES*
  Jeff Fountain
  Initial Media, 2007

- *THESE FIFTEEN*
  Edwin Sayer
  Comenius Press, 1963

- *THROUGH FIVE HUNDRED YEARS AND BEYOND*
  Allen W. Schattschneider and Albert H. Frank
  Comenius Press, revised edition 2007

- *WILLIAM CAREY*
  James Culross
  Hodder & Stoughton, 1881

- *WILLIAM CAREY*
  Janet & Geoff Benge
  YWAM Publishing, 2004

- *YOU ARE MY WITNESSES*
  James Weingarth
  Inter-Provincial Women's Board, Moravian Church, 1981

- *ZINZENDORF, THE ECUMENICAL PIONEER*
  A.J. Lewis
  SCM, 1962

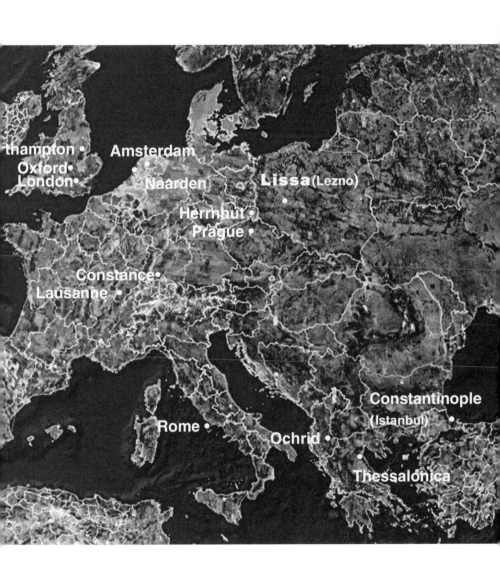

POLAND

•Goerlitz

• Bautzen

HERRNHUT • •Berthelsdorf

10 km

• Zittau

C Z E C H   R E P U B L I C

To learn more about the exciting lives of other figures in History who

'pressed on toward the goal for the prize
of the upward call of God in Christ Jesus'
(Phil 3:14)

Then come explore the following biography series' :

Christian Heroes: Then & Now
By Janet & Geoff Benge

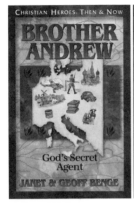
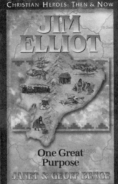

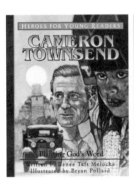
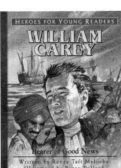
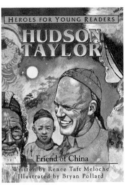

Heroes for Young Readers
Written by Renee Taft Meloche – Illustrated by Bryan Pollard